Salty Liquor

by

Gary Rainford

Salty Liquor

Copyright © 2014 by Gary Rainford

All rights reserved. No part of this book may be reproduced or transmitted in any form or by any means without written permission of the author.

ISBN 978-0-945980-86-5

Library of Congress Control Number: 2014955452

Cover photo by Ann Marie Maguire

for Mimi, my wife, my compass

Acknowledgments

Thanks to the editors of the following publications where some of the poems in this collection, or earlier versions, originally appeared:

"Smolder," in *Roundupzine*, Vol. 2-1, 2014

"Burnt Coat Harbor," in *The Island Reader, Vol. IX* (Spring 2014)

"Sundown," in *Blast Furnace Volume 4, Issue 1*, 2014

"Let Me Have It," as "Payback is a Spiky Purple Lupine" in a "Featured Author" interview at *Roundupzine*, Fall 2014

"After Book Club," in *Kindred*, Fall 2013

"Thunder Hole," "Clover," & "No Rest for the Weary," in *Omphalos 12*, Summer / Fall 2011

"Evolution," in *The Aputamkon Review*, Vol. IV, 2011

"Localvores," in *Red Line Blues 8*, 2011

"Rites of Passage," *Words and Images* (University of Southern Maine), 2010

"Hieroglyphics," *The Aurorean*, Spring / Summer 2010

"Ducks," *The Island Reader*, Vol. IV, 2009

"Artifice," in *Wavelength: Poems in Prose and Verse*, Summer 2008

"Wintering," "Open Season," & "Fists, Charm, Humanity,"
North Dakota Quarterly, Winter 2008

Table of Contents

Low Tide / 1
Localvores / 2
After Book Club / 3
Evolution / 4
Man-Made / 5
Predator, Teeth Bared / 6
Open Season / 7
Thunder Hole / 9
Fists, Charm, Humanity / 11
Hieroglyphics / 12
Rites of Passage / 13
Let Me Have It / 15
A Harvard Club Lecture / 16
Headin' Upcamp / 17
Frostbite / 18
Wintering / 19
Scattered Ashes in Frenchman Bay / 20
One Foot in the Grave / 21
Groundhog's Almanac / 22
A Tarot Reading / 23
Smoke Signals / 24
Ducks / 25
Nocturne / 26
So Far, So Good / 27
Anemometer / 28
Smolder / 29
Dutch Treat / 30
Quahog / 31
Checkers / 32

Stay-at-Home Dad / 33
Bread and Cheese Spread Man / 35
Loose Change / 37
Marco Polo / 38
Philadelphia, Market East Station / 39
Burnt Coat Harbor / 40
Artifice / 41
Family Reunion / 42
Godevil / 43
Magnetic North / 44
Clover / 45
Miss Shrew / 46
Torrey Beach / 47
Prayer Vigil / 48
Qualifications / 49
No Rest for the Weary / 50
Sundown / 51

FOREWORD

Last night after book-club I reversed my pickup truck into a ditch—not intentionally / My mother is forgetful / Scott, my older brother, called two weeks ago / He is a sign maker / Driving home from Bangor yesterday a Ford Fusion, heading into oncoming traffic, beeped twice while passing me / RU NICE, asked his vanity license plate, which made me smile and say to myself, "I can be" / My daughter, Meri, says, "I love you, Daddy," when she wakes up from a bad dream / Her mother and I have the same tattoo, a black, thick-lined wave.

Waves are interesting. Think about it; no two waves are the same, yet every wave is connected to a greater marine system, the ocean. Waves are individual, yet dependent. As a symbol of our marriage, and to celebrate ten years, we storied our bodies. My next tattoo will be a compass, the navigational type, not the instrument used for drawing circles.

What does all this have to do with *Salty Liquor?* Stories. I use poetry to tell stories. I've been telling stories since I was a boy drawing cartoons. When I was hospitalized for asthma, the summer after 6th grade, sitting upright to cartoon the nurses made my chest rattle like wind chimes. That's when I began writing poetry. First in my head. Then on paper.

Everybody has stories. Everybody has poetry. My wife or I read to Meri every day, and she reads to us now too, chapter books. She'll stall at bedtime by asking how to say a new word. "Energy," her mother pronounced the other night, and Meri's face lighted up.

I love words, the music, every shape and shadow, and how
they tumble and jump and fall; my brother is a sign maker,
                       and words, like signs, point us
                       in every conceivable
                       and inconceivable direction.

       --Gary Rainford, Swan's Island, Maine, 2014

"When you start to doubt yourself the real world will eat you alive."

--Henry Rollins

Low Tide

The smell of fish. A seagull searches
the black clumps of seaweed teeming with sand fleas;
she picks out a choice mussel with her beak,
flies straight up, white wings trembling,
then drops it on the rocks below. It takes
three tries to crack open the mussel
shell before she can suck out the sweet meat,
the salty liquor.

Localvores

You gather the last few fresh carrots
from a fish tote
that keeps all winter
in your cellar.
Stack them in a stainless steel colander
painted white, the fecund smell
of manure, sharp. The moist loam,
mud between your fingers.
Sue puts up a bushel for you from her garden,
six or eight layers
of carrots and moss as wadding
that she collects
from the other side of the island;
her mother-in-law gets a bushel for canning;
and what doesn't rot by the cold,
hard rains in November
Sue blanches, then freezes
in trim, vacuum sealed,
quart pouches.
But you prefer the ceremony:
heading back upstairs to the kitchen;
scrubbing an epoch of dirt
off each one;
slicing them into piles of orange coins.
And for a split second,
when the June of last year's carrots sizzle
in a cast iron skillet
spitting butter,
the seasons are as sacred
as places.

After Book Club

We pull into the driveway.
It's late for Meri on a school night.
She's excited to be awake

past bedtime; we step out
of the car, and the moon, not quite full
until tomorrow, catches us

off guard. Sue's garden is lit up
like corned hake, and in the tall grass
of sky and the oncoming traffic

of autumn, Meri poets, "The leaves--
eenie meenie miney moe--
look like stars on the ground."

Evolution

It's not raining, but a dense fog is falling
heavy in the trees, and it feels like rain, as if you are standing
stark naked on the muddy banks of the Amazon,
or chasing feral pigs in the Daintree, or being chased
by devils in the cloud forest of Equator,
but you're not; you're Downeast, coastal Maine,
middle of the night, tossing steamer shells
and lobster parts picked clean for the compost you keep
by an old foundation where a barn once
stood.

Man-Made

"Are you making your daughter a dress?"
an attractive young woman in her 20s with purple streaks
in her hair asks.

I am standing with Meri at the cutting table
at Walmart; I am holding a bolt
of sparkly red fabric she picked out, eyeballing whether
we'll need one or two yards.

"Is your daddy making you a dress?" she raises a pierced brow
and eyes Meri this time.

"Not a dress," I reply. "A skirt. I promised my daughter
I'd make her a skirt to wear at the ballet.

"That's the sweetest," she slow motion scans my arms covered
with tattoos and gives her breasts a heartfelt pat.

Predator, Teeth Bared

Driving past the fireponds
an eagle lifts off from Atlantic Road
blooming of the copious scrub,
alders and pitch pines.

Black wings stretch across an ox cart
of two lanes. I speed up.

A gray rabbit hangs limp and dying
in the eagle's rip-talons.

I am in awe. Where I grew up
nature was topiary, mowed lawns, and
chain link fences.

"Look, Meri!" says her mother
pointing. "What kind of animal is that?"

"Predator!" Meri snaps, teeth bared.

Open Season

A four door, 1980's, Monte Carlo sedan, battered
to hell, creeps down Atlantic Road, then back up again.

The driver and two passengers scope and measure
the distance, rifles pointed
out half open windows wishing for that perfect deer,
that perfect kill.

It's nearly dusk. Red brake lights flicker, hold,
flicker, hold . . .

I am standing in the dooryard, alone, but in the woods
behind my house a murder
of crows has been screaming and fighting
for hunger all day, pecking what's left
of the rotting deer flesh, the bloodied fur, the bones,
the vacant eye sockets.

"Three days," I whisper and make a gun with my fingers
and thumb.

"Three more days of open season,"
I pull the cold trigger, and yesterday, we were standing
over a dead deer carcass like crime scene
examiners.

"Right here," Sput said, and he shifted the six point buck
by his proud antlers. "Looks like a .22 caliber
to me. A clean shot, right through the shoulder,
and what a waste."

Spencer agreed, shaking his head, troubled
that poachers would forfeit so much good Island meat
to crows, and then he asked if I had heard any gunshots
after dark lately.

"All the time," I nodded, and like mourners
at a graveside Mass we stood there blank as cordwood,
this rural country of treetops, this rural country
of saltwater.

Thunder Hole

A seven year old girl
on vacation
is sucked into Thunder Hole
by a seventeen foot wave
the day after Hurricane Bill
lands on Mount Desert
Island. I don't ever
want to know the terror
she must have felt
or her father's gagging misery
hours later when she is pulled
from the seawater,
unresponsive,
cold as 55 degrees Fahrenheit,
cold as dead. It is inconceivable:
the cell phone calls
he had to make,
the voicemail he had to leave,
the texts, *CALL ME*,
only a trembling hand
could explain,
and then, driving home
to New York City,
his wife
in the passenger seat,
the stain of her greatest
heartbreak
marked on the skin by now

like a tattoo,
like the indelible blot
I also carry around
for my first daughter,
the day I held her
in my arms
for more than two hours
while she died,
every dream she'd ever invent
awash, buried in the silty,
saltwater of birth
and surging back to the sea
where she was just
pulled from
between her mother's
quivering legs.

Fists, Charm, Humanity

Southwest out of Blue Hill Bay thin fog moves in,
high tide across Atlantic Road.

Spotlights of sun split trees
into shadows.

Mid-morning. The Eastern Way is a plantation
of lobstermen setting gear.

It's windy. Knee-high meadow grasses sweep my legs
and hiss. A snake uncoils, springs away.

Two wing-stretched eagles swimming
dip into currents of salt-air
and squawk like terror. They see me. I am bigger,
but they are gods.

Fists, charm, and humanity are no match against claws
and wild, stinging beaks.

Hieroglyphics

Meri dips two fingers
into the small, quick moving stream.
"Draw-ing," she replies

looking up at her mother,
her toddler voice clipped and tectonic
as a blessing,

and she paints another masterpiece
of blotchy lines and wet handprints as if
to understate the obvious: *I am here,
I have so much to say.*

Rites of Passage

I am stretched out on the pine floor,
wet sanding the areas
where five coats of tung oil resin
formed hard, gritty pearls,
not smooth glass, like the online video
pledged.

WKIT, Stephen King's rock and roll station,
is tuned in on the radio,
Foghat belting out, "Slow Ride."

The blue, sunny sky day reminds me
of Marty, a high school friend, who had just
passed the exam for his junior license,
which meant he could drive almost anywhere,
to school and work, to his girlfriend's,
even Jones Beach, but his car, a 1975, two door,
Chevy clunker, had to be home and
parked by sunset, by curfew.

For weeks, we banged out dents;
we scrubbed away rust with wire brushes;
smeared cans of creamy Bondo
to every square inch practically; and then,
like sculptors, we wet sanded
and smoothed all the rough, gray patches
to near perfection; and one morning,

the sun and cicadas screaming, Marty asked
if I knew how to buy, "linga-re."

"Buy what?" I replied, turning the
word, "linga-re," over and over
in my head, thinking how it rhymed
with dungaree.

"You know," he said. "Sexy
underwear. The lacy stuff. Me and Denise's
one year anniversary's next week."

"Marty," I snorted, "it's *lingerie*, not
'linga-re.' Stick to flowers, dude. Boxes of
chocolates. I don't think you're ready
for 'linga-re.' "

We laughed like monkeys, and Marty
finally had the car painted blue.

Let Me Have It

We'd dogfight in the empty aerobics room
after working out
at the YMCA, an audience of mirrors chanting,
"Pain!"

Thirty years later I'm an adjunct college
professor of English, and my brother is taking
a college course, his first.

We still joke on the phone
about my fractured tailbone, how he body-slammed
the concrete floor covered of yoga mats,
and the blood-thirsty meat hook that broke
my molar.

He sends multiple email attachments now,
drafts of his essays.

"Okay, Professor," he'll write, "let me have it;
payback's a bitch."

A Harvard Club Lecture

"Where's my hug?" chirps Meri,
groggy as a unicorn, the light of my cellphone tunneling
predawn darkness.

According to a recent study, Gen Xers, the alleged *slacker*
generation, spend more time working, making ends
meet, than our parents, yet we manage to spend more
time with our children.

The same study concludes that my daughter's generation,
the *quiet*, overprotected generation,
isn't developing the cognitive processes necessary
to make decisions on their own.

"Where are you going?" Meri chirps, again, the bottom stair
skreaking. "I invented a new hug."

Headin' Upcamp

"Look at us!" I turn the key in the ignition
and Bert fastens the seatbelt over his puffy down coat;
the parking lot at Hannaford's is Monday, busy
and bustling.

"We are real men!" I grunt like Tim Allen
from *Last Man Standing*, all sorts of gear packed in the back,
snowshoes, boots, a cooler, bags of groceries,
wine and booze, a snow shovel in case Tuesday's storm
gets that crazy February look in its eyes.

"Yessir," Bert plays along and jokes. "We are
Headin' upcamp. To write poetry and make paintings.
A couple of true wild men."

I discovered Thoreau's, *Walden,* in college,
Professor Nelson's 19th Century Literature course. Jocelyn
always sat in front of me. She was grunge
before Nirvana and Pearl Jam got air play on MTV.
"I went to the woods because I wished to live deliberately,
to front only the essential facts of life," she wrote
in my notebook quoting Thoreau. I was a junior and
switched my major from computer science
to literature.

"Thank God," I laugh with Bert and shift the truck
into reverse. "A hundred times thank God we're not going
ice fishing!"

Frostbite

Working his rotation on the Henry Lee,
Bob hauls rope by hand, clumps of frozen seaweed
muck, ice like fire.

As we pull into the ferry slip, bucking,
the wind scrapes Mackerel Cove, and a slurry of saltwater
sorbet skins the hull.

Bob strips off a pair of soaked, useless gloves. His
hands are numb, somebody else's.

Wintering

It's early. A gaunt morning moon
is a frozen hole
in the gray, still sky.

The Captain Henry Lee, our ferry,
won't be crossing today.

The island, cut off, locked down,
is without electricity. Or telephone.

Giant and collapsed ice heaves
like megaliths
clutter Mackerel Cove.

The roads are frozen. Snowdrifts
are frozen. Deep, artesian well
casings are frozen. Domestic hot water
pipes are frozen. Septic lines, frozen.
Gas lines, frozen solid, too,
and my pickup truck wouldn't start
last Friday.

Buddy at the dump described oil
in his Cherokee as slushy.

January doesn't thaw
until the very first purple crocus bulb
blooms in May.

Scattered Ashes in Frenchman Bay

I force my left foot into the snowshoe binding,
wade thigh deep snow around the orange
no trespass warning tape blocking the *Sundew* gazebo
trailhead.

Fresh powder twists and turns through a narrow
of salt granite spruce where deer and rabbit tracks point
the way west to Frenchman Bay.

"I'm not sure this is safe," I call out
to nobody, and walk off the trail into the white, crack
of ageless time crushing the shoreline.

My neighbor died last night, liver, heart,
and kidney failure. He was sick for years and a sad story
since his wife died.

I used to help him lift what he couldn't
anymore, boxes marked New Jersey, a motorized chair
for Georgia when she started stumbling
down stairs, deck furniture, a wood lathe, empty propane
tanks, a treadmill . . . .

Stepping closer to the edge I wash snow and
seaweed from frosted crampons. I peel off my gloves,
reach down. The saltwater is lethal. I am happy
for Ken, and once my hands quit stinging, I wave goodbye
and say a prayer, sort of, for us all.

One Foot in the Grave

"Lately, out the corner of my eye,
when I'm waking up, I see her
ghost," says my mother talking about Grandma,
dead over thirty years.

"I think I'm dreaming, but I'm not;
it's actually her standing in my bedroom, facing
the wall, gathering the distance.

"She wants me to follow,
or something like you said, 'take her hand and
no more pain.'

"Plus, I didn't tell you, I see Grandpa
too, dancing, whooping it up. Singing old Italian
songs.

"That's all he ever wanted, to be
with people he loved. I think he's saying
dead's a party.

"After physical therapy," my mother changes
the subject, her voice old, a weary mix
of cellphone static and panic, "it can take a year,
you know, before I'm fully recovered,
not three weeks, not hip surgery, but I have pots
and pans, lots of good ones, expensive
cookware I can't part with. Do you want
my Pyrex?"

Groundhog's Almanac

"Have a good day," I say to Clay.

We are pulling into the ferry slip.
It's cold, chunks of ice
in the harbor scrape the hull.

"That reminds me," Clay smiles
adjusting thick winter gloves. "I read
a bumper sticker just recently,
'A Good Day is Any Day Above
Ground.' "

"That's one way to live, I suppose,"
I reply.

"Above ground is the only way
to live," Clay laughs, zips
up his jacket, the sky moody, clouded
over like the promissory note
of early spring.

A Tarot Reading

One of the first games we play is Memory,
finding the most pairs of picture cards. At the library
my daughter and I played endless matches
of the Disney edition. There are so many new characters
since I was a kid: Aladdin, Bolt, Brave, Ariel,
Mulan, Lilo & Stitch.

I asked my mother if she played match games
growing up in the 1940s. She remembered an oversized
stack of flashcards Grandma kept
wrapped in a swatch of delicate cloth and bound
altogether by thick red rubber bands.

"Hearts, the sun, a horse, an old magician,
kings and queens, a monk, pointed stars, a smiling moon,
dancing skeletons, a lion's cub," she reminisced
but she doesn't always remember which side of the road
to drive on either, or the difference between junk
mail and the phone bill.

Smoke Signals

Theo McCormick lives at Sonogee now,
a senior residence
for people with long-term care needs.

Theo's husband died last year,
maybe two years ago. You lose track
of time.

My neighbors and I pass their empty house
in Atlantic every day.

When my wife says let's take a vacation
as a family, Paris, Prague, or the
moon, I see the prickly sow-thistle blooming
yellow in the clay packed driveway,

where the McCormicks' Camry is rooted
like a headstone, and the news of their vanity
license plate, WRLDS2C, climbs up
the sky two puffs of smoke.

Ducks

My daughter and I skip and run
a quarter mile
to the fireponds in Atlantic.

"Duck," she points,
then puts her hands up in the air,
like a question, and shrugs.

Nested in the reeds and grasses
growing back sparsely
along the gray, clay waterline
a mallard has been missing
since spring, since the fire
department dredged and widened
the fireponds.

"I don't know where
the duck went," I shake my head,
plunging my hands
in the air like hers. "He is someplace
else, now. Someplace . . . safer,
not so . . . ," but before I can finish
guessing, about the world,
these fireponds, Meri is
already sidetracked,
little fingers stabbing the dirt
road.

Nocturne

"Whooo, Whooo,
Whooo?" asks the owl
nesting in a copse
of birch, and the rain
answers.

So Far, So Good

"Are you sure?" my mother mewls
into the phone, uncertain whether it's morning
or 6:40 at night, and then we're stopped
in traffic, singing, "Row, Row, Row, Your Boat,"
as a round.

I am my daughter's age, seven, and the Chevy
rust-bucket stalls. "Oh, shit!"
my mother cranks the motor twice.

You don't recognize the initial stages
of dementia like you recognize the knocking engine,
the blue smoke, the failed state emissions
inspection.

"Is Mom okay now?" I ask
two hours later when my stepfather answers
the phone.

"So far, so good," he says, no hint of sarcasm, no
humor in his voice.

Anemometer

The wind's howl, savage,
picks up force and speed as it cuts across Blue Hill
Bay, whipsaws Atlantic Road,
rams my house, rattles it, the walls, the windows,
the block foundation nearly two centuries old,
then keeps moving, no conscience, no guilt, no more pity
than a sunrise.

Smolder

Toxic brown chemicals smolder
choke the hallway
between our bedrooms. I open my door enough to see
my brother dragging a piss-stained mattress
into the stairwell. "If you tell Mom, you're dead,"
he grunts.

Our mother slept through most of it
or overlooked the obvious, the all night binges, the drugs,
the drug runs, the bottles of piss.

"I must'f dropped a cigarette," his girlfriend tongues
the air, eyes thin cracks, body of slum
methadone maintenance. "Now go back to sleep," she nods,
bony fingers shooing me.

In the morning, outside,
the metal frame of the mattress is all that is left
standing behind the garage,
the springs still warm and seething when I spray them
with the hose.

Dutch Treat

"You don't have to eat it," I say to myself,
scraping my daughter's bowl of leftover Cheerios
into a bucket we use for composting.

I can hear my grandfather's instructions,
Take as much bread as you want, but eat what you take,
he'd fork the air.

My mother is overweight. You can visit a lifetime
battle with food by cleaning out her kitchen
cabinets: Weight Watchers lemon cakes, Jenny Craig skinny
bars, cans of expired Slimfast,
and all those appetite suppressing pills that rhyme
with acetylene.

"Hey, Dad," says Meri. "Next time we're off-island
can we get ice cream at Blueberry Hill?"

"Absolutely!" I lick the honeyed spoon, a believer
in *All Things Moderation*.

Quahog

Jimmy reaches into the open
tailgate. "I got a bucket of quahogs,
if you want 'em?"

"Are you serious!?" I reply,
but Jimmy just fists a clam and launches
another one into the pine woods.

As a boy, I'd wade up to my waist
at Jones Beach State Park,
the muddy bay across from the causeway
tower. "Another landmine,"
I'd yell and dig one out of the muck
with gritty toes.

My mom cooked chowders
or baked clams casino, breaded paprika
crowns.

Walking home I can taste
the garlic, Jimmy's spackle bucket
brimming.

Checkers

"Life," my daughter crickets
in her sleep.

My grandmother used to joke

about a time when I was four, Meri's age,
playing crazy in the backyard
all by myself, devoured by the sun, lost
to introspection.

"What are you doing?"
Gram coughs from the screen door,
her smoker's voice raspy
like rust.

"Working out," I pump skinny biceps,
smear sweat across my forehead,
and shake like a mystic; I am trying to move
a rock with my inner essence.

"You have to be strong, Gram,
to beat the world at checkers," I tense and
strain.

"Life," my daughter crickets
in her sleep.

Stay-at-Home Dad

"What are you doing?" I ask, calm as mint tea,
although I am caught off guard:

Meri is standing in the middle of our kitchen;
purple-red sunset skirt hiked up
to her neck; and the snowflake tights I helped her into
this morning heaped around both ankles;

her expression, shame and necessity,
stabs my heart. "It's okay," I kneel down, reassure her.
"But what's the matter?"

"I have itches," Meri struggles, "inside
my cracks."

"Oh, that's an easy fix," I reply,
but when I nudge her Hello Kitty underpants down,
she pounces,

"Daddy, I tried already, and my arm's too short!
See!?"

Playing along, I take her hand in mine, inspect
the length of each knuckle, like you'd eyeball 2X4s
at Home Depot.

"Just as I thought," I nod. "Your itch-to-reach ratio is out
of whack."

"My what?"

"Give me your other hand," I point and shake both arms
like gobs of taffy. "That'll do it."

"Thanks, Daddy," she scratches now and giggles
like a ragdoll.

"You're welcome," I reply, guiding her
by the elbow to the bathroom sink, "but let's wash hands
first with soap before we touch anything
else."

Bread and Cheese Spread Man

The bread and cheese spread man at Sam's Club
cuts Meri a fat chunk of fluffy fresh bread.

"She's your big helper, huh?" he says
but you don't reply, you smile and nod instead,
too busy for chitchat.

"She'll be off to college or married
before you know it," he persists
even though you are halfway down the aisle
trundling toward the great wall
of refrigerated meats.

"It's amazing how fast time flies,"
the bread and cheese spread man's voice booms
over all the other store chatter.

You have a choice, but you don't want
to be rude, so you ask the bread and cheese
spread man how old his daughters are,
and he says, one's 25, and one's 28, but he winces
when he tells you what a heartbreaker it is
when they grow up and move away.

"I'm not looking forward to it,"
is your passing reply, fingers scanning

expiration dates on discounted packages of strip
steak.

"Only one thing's harder," he levels
pencil sharp eyes over rim-thick, black glasses,
and it seems as if he and you are the only
two people in the entire store, now.

"What's that?" you ask, unexpectedly curious,
heading back to his table.

"When they don't grow up, when they don't move
away," the bread and cheese spread man
shrugs, then brushes the breast of his starched,
white apron.

Loose Change

In 1946 Eva filed three poems with Burton's
lobster slips. Each years' worth
of receipts were bundled into shoe boxes and stored
in the attic.

"Nobody's Child" is about an outcast,
a beggar with "no father, no mother, no sister, not one."
Her dress is ragged, yet a "great world of light"
opens the sky, like a gate.

"Somebody's Mother" is about an old,
gray woman "bent with the chill of the winter's day."
She is stranded in a snowbank, invisible to all
the young men who pass-her-by. Then a soldier gallops in
to "lend a hand."

"The Tale of a Tramp" is about grief,
a blacksmith from Lehigh Valley, whose sixteen year
old daughter, Nellie, elopes with a "city chap."
Months later, at her mother's bedside, Nellie dies
of heartbreak.

All three poems are handwritten, anonymous,
and folded neatly into thirds. The stationery is thin
as tissue paper, the words, fading pencil lines,
cursive swoops. When Jimmy came over to show me
I thought he said, "Look at Mother's old
coins."

Marco Polo

My daughter's little fingers, tight knuckles, lock
mine into place; we are 150,000 pounds roaring into the sky,
jet engines vibrating the fuselage.

The woman in front of us can't relax;
her bottle of Schweppes darts
off the empty seat beside her, rolls down the center aisle,
and my eyes follow
that thin strip of floor-lights to the emergency door
where you can't avoid the breaking news:
two pings were discovered today, a global game of Marco Polo,
coming from the black box
of the missing without a trace, Malaysia Airlines,
Flight 370.

Philadelphia, Market East Station

"Can you hit me up with a dollar
for the train?" asks a short, middle aged guy
a few years younger than me.

At a glance he's all business,
heading home after a day at work, blue suit
coat, brown loafers, but the tank-top
and too long sweatpants tell a different story.

"Thanks," he says when I hold the public
restroom door open, so he can enter,
but I can tell by the glassy recognition in his eyes
that I'm the asshole who ignored him
five minutes ago.

I reach into my pocket, pull out two
dollars. "Life is hard from everybody," I snap,
hand dryers roaring, toilets flushing.

Burnt Coat Harbor

Seagulls are constants.
High and low tides are constants. Blue sky
is constant. The saltwater is.
The sun that inspires the harbor
to do great work is constant. The craggy
coastline. Every passing cloud.

Meri is playing on the swings
at Mill Pond Park, and I am steadfast,
a ferryboat anchored off her shore.

Constants. The site of Hockomock Head Lighthouse
when Samuel de Champlain
sailed the area in 1604
was a pockmark of Indian campfires,
so he called the hill, *brules cote, burnt coast*,
to set apart Swan's Island
from other islands.

Constants. They keep us on course.

"Swing me higher, Daddy!" Meri squawks,
so I swing her higher
and thank God for the constant attention
she demands.

Artifice

Black Rock Beach greets a receded shoreline.
Boulders, like sculptures, measure time
by standing still. A tight belt of gangly pine trees surround
the outer slopes in a semicircle,

anchor this private cove. Seagulls, like lobster
buoys, drift and rise over calm, bantam
swells, and the air, a saltwater stew, is ebullient: dead sea
urchins, disemboweled crabs and scattered parts,
abandoned periwinkle shells, muscles cracked open and picked
clean, seaweed teeming with fleas and life, sponge-bed
mosses, barnacles, rich musty mud ancient
as God,

and humidity. You spot and pick up a rock. It is a jewel,
black as despair, shiny as a wish, smooth as polish.
You spot another,

and another. You have a fistful of priceless jewels.
You gather them in your shirt. Dry them. A tiny bit of
perfection rubs off,

yet they are still special. Walking home you turn them
over in your hands like rosary beads, sacred
and blessed, but when you get to Atlantic Road, they are dull
and ordinary; they are so transformed you shrug and
toss them over your shoulder.

Family Reunion

In high school kids called me cocaine
eyes because mine were set in dark bruised
sockets.

I didn't know I had Granddad's eyes
until I was 45, when a cousin posted his picture
on Facebook.

He died when our fathers were boys.

Seeing his face was reunion, like finding light
before the sky had blue.

Godevil

It's cold, negative teens,
and the fresh snow is a pool of sun so sharp
it burns your eyes.

When my stepbrother Jim slams the ax
head down, it bounces back.

"Don't be afraid of it," says Jim senior,
his father, in his seventies, still strong for a man
with heart trouble, hands like mauls.

"Yeah, don't be a pussy," I fan the fire, streaks of
gray in my beard like icicles.

Jim looks up. "That's what I heard, too,"
he shakes his head as if
nothing has changed for twenty five years since
we last saw each other.

Magnetic North

Meri counts eight deer.
She is kneeling on the couch, gazing out the window,
each finger a placeholder.

My stepfather gave me a gift.
As a boy, we spent Memorial Day weekends upstate,
New York, near the Canadian border.
The drive was long, but a watchfulness busied our time
once the Adirondack mountains appeared
at dawn, bold and bottomless
compared to the subdivision where we lived.

"Can I take a picture, Daddy?"
Meri has that look of awe on her face, too, a compass, magnetic
north to help find her way.

Clover

Unfocus your eyes. Let the day go fuzzy.

White cottonheads of clover. Swarming.
Supply nectar, bees with pollen.

Lobster boat engines rumble the seashore.
Speak to granite.

Aches and pains and sunshine serenade July.

The wind. Buoyant. Warms your lips.

Three eagles pass overhead. One shrieks.

When you know your way in the blur. In
the out-of-focus. The path is lit with honey.

Miss Shrew

It's a cold, chill morning in May.
I follow Meri, whirling and speechless, to a nook
underneath the staircase.

Trapped inside a jar
a velvety shrew, smaller than my big toe, is dying,
but holding to life like petals of roses
to a cut stem.

When I palm the jar, tiny shrew feet struggle,
then fall. And when she lifts her shrew head, red eyes
are delusions.

Meri feels so terrible we let Miss Shrew go
loose in the yard, way out back by the honeysuckle
vines where other shrews and mice seem to like
the hotel of tall grasses.

"I want Miss Shrew to live, see another sunrise,"
Meri points at the sky.

"Go shrew, go shrew, go," I get down on my knees
and elbows, but she hardly moves.

Torrey Beach

We are parked on the dirt road
at the old airstrip.

I roll down Meri's window, turn off
the car.

White capped waves pound the shore.

You feel their muscle and bulk
in your bones like memories.

As far back as I remember
the foreign language of ocean
had influence.

Boulders. Sand. Saltwater. Tides.

"Daddy," Meri points at a giant
screaming wave,
jetting up like a fountain,
"what's it saying?"

"I don't know," I tell her, "but one day
maybe you will
speak Torrey Beach and translate
for Daddy."

Prayer Vigil

Thunder rumbles, cracks September
open like a geode. Inside, crystals of lightening flash,
shake the sky white. Deer hiss and fuss
undercover of spruce

and wild grasses; a spotted fawn, clumsy hooves
circles Atlantic road, then bolts. Charismatic crickets
chirping, deliver a chance, seaside

sermon. The rain. The buoyant, salt breeze, and my
wife and daughter trekking downstairs
to the bathroom while the Island asleep dreams,

ripe mackerel stuffed bait bags, lobster traps brimming,
the squabbles of gulls.

Qualifications

"I have a job for you,"
I say to Meri
before she plops on the couch.

"No, thanks," she replies.

"What do you mean, 'No,
thanks?'" I dump an armload of birch
in the woodbox.

"Okay, what's the job?"

"Barney needs food,
fresh water—rinse out his bowl
please—and a chew treat."

"No, thanks. I don't have
the qualifications for that," she shrugs,
walks away, and I wonder,

What did Jacques d'Arc think
about his daughter

before she inspired the world, or
Samuel Edwin Stanton

Earhart, or Oprah's dad?

No Rest for the Weary

Steady, predawn rain
gentle as a guru's mantra.

You hear the sweetest voices
landing on the blue tarps
you wrestled with in the wind yesterday
to cover a truckload of studs
and the pine boards
piled across the mud-splattered
driveway.

You stay in bed this morning
to listen. To remember how perfectly
the sound of rain
lifts your spirit, drives out confusion.

A meditation. Every raindrop.
The puddles that have no place
to drain.

Sundown

Snow and sleet
dumped from the sky
at intervals.

By sundown drifts
of dense accumulation
rippled and rolled
out

across the field
where deer find refuge
by a congregation

of gnarled
and heirloom apple
trees.

When you looked,
the light was so thin
you could spin it

around your fingers
and be in a million different
places at once or be

a million different
people. Or be yourself.
Here.

About the Author

Gary Rainford lives on Swan's Island year-round with his wife and daughter. His poetry, shaped by tides and saltwater, is published in a wide range of literary magazines and university journals, including *North Dakota Quarterly, Words and Images, Aurorean, Omphalos, Kindred*, and *Blast Furnace*. Gary was a featured poet on the Maine Poetry Express, at *The Roundup Writer's Zine,* and Artist-in-Residence in Acadia National Park. Gary grew up on Long Island, NY, but home is six miles off the north coast of Maine where rocks, wind, eagles, sky, spruce trees, and seasons converge on the sprawling field outside his office window. Interested in Gary's work? Connect with him at www.garyrainford.com.

www.ingramcontent.com/pod-product-compliance
Lightning Source LLC
Chambersburg PA
CBHW051716040426
42446CB00008B/907